P9-ELR-075

HOW TO

TRAUMATIZE
YOUR CHILDREN

**KNOCK
KNOCK**®
knockknockstuff.com

Created and published by

Knock Knock
11111 Jefferson Blvd. #5167
Culver City, CA 90231
knockknockstuff.com

© 2011 Knock Knock LLC
All rights reserved
Knock Knock is a registered trademark of Knock Knock LLC
Made in China

Illustrated by Bradley R. Hughes

No part of this product may be used or reproduced in any manner
whatsoever without prior written permission from the publisher,
except in the case of brief quotations embodied in critical articles
and reviews. For information, address Knock Knock.

This book is a work of humor meant solely for entertainment pur-
poses. It is not intended to recommend or advise regarding how to
raise children. The advice contained in this book is intended as
a parody of parenting and psychology books; actually following
the advice contained herein will not be good for children. The
publisher and anyone associated with the production of this book
do not advocate child abuse or breaking the law. In no event will
Knock Knock be liable to any reader for any damages, including
direct, indirect, incidental, special, consequential, or punitive
damages, arising out of or in connection with the use of the information contained in this book. So there.

Every reasonable attempt has been made to identify owners of
copyright. Errors or omissions will be corrected in subsequent
editions.

Where specific company, product, and brand names are cited,
copyright and trademarks associated with these names are prop-
erty of their respective owners.

ISBN: 978-160106309-0
UPC: 825703-50004-2

CONTENTS

TRAUMA WITH A PURPOSE

1

INTRODUCTION

All children need a steady dose of trauma in order
to conduct therapy-worthy adult lives. While
most—if not all—parents traumatize their children
accidentally, the fact that you're reading this book
shows you love your kids so much that you'll screw
them up deliberately and with skill. Rather than
mindlessly repeating the trauma that was visited
upon you by your own parents, you know the value
of seeking improvement from one generation
to the next. You understand that children need
psychological peril they can take with them into
adulthood and all future relationships, and you

care enough to do it yourself. With this book and a bit of focus, you'll be traumatizing your children in no time. You'll learn:

- How the advantages of childhood trauma will benefit your children.

- Dynamics common to most traumatic parenting and how to amplify them in your own parent-child interactions.

> ### Tidings of Trauma
>
> *"If you have never been hated by your child, you have never been a parent."*
>
> **—Bette Davis**

- How to play to your own strengths in choosing a particular traumatizing approach, based on your natural inclinations and behavioral style.

- What outcomes to expect in your children, both immediately and when they grow into adulthood.

Trauma Denial:
It's Not Just a River in Egypt

The secret truth of trauma is that *all* children are traumatized, no matter their parents' efforts to the contrary. The differences between in-advertently traumatizing your children and doing so purposefully are as follows:

- You will choose your traumatizing style based on your family's needs rather than defaulting into it by instinct.

- The trauma will be more skillfully applied, with midcourse corrections possible thanks to self-awareness.

- Because trauma is inevitable, you won't spin in circles of self-recrimination as you attempt to avoid it.

- Unhampered by denial, you won't be surprised when your children turn out to be screwed up. Rather than asking "Where did I go wrong?" you'll know exactly what you did right.

"My Parents Were Crazy": The Many Benefits of Trauma

The traumatized child becomes a rich, flavorful adult, equipped with resources that untraumatized or mistraumatized children don't possess. While your child may initially rebel against your traumatizing style, someday he will not only be grateful, he will possibly choose to replicate it with his own offspring. Even if you already believe in the importance of trauma, you will no doubt encounter naysayers and know-it-alls, so it's always useful to be equipped with as many counterarguments as possible.

Your Child Will Fit In

Because everybody is traumatized in childhood, your child will experience belonging and acceptance. During adolescence, for example, your child could forge friendships of rebellion, experimenting with sex, drugs, and piercings alongside her peers. In adulthood, your child will be able to discuss with friends his repetitive dysfunctional relationships, wondering aloud why it is that he seeks out the same noncommittal bimbos over and over again.

Your Child Will Have Character

Regular adversity is like a ThighMaster for the inner self, and the strength arising from trauma is a hallmark of the successfully screwed-up adult. The rare child who has not been traumatized has trouble handling the realities of a cruel world, and may crumble at the first sign of trouble. The traumatized child, on the other hand, meets the world with well-developed muscles, prepared with such tools as selfishness, lack of boundaries, or a tough outer shell. Despite idealized notions to the contrary, a traumatized child is a prepared child.

Your Child Will Have Something to Rebel Against—You!

Not all traumatizing approaches result in rebellion, but many do. What object is better to rebel against than a loving parent? In addition to being a virtually universal rite of passage, rebellion allows your child to experiment with alternate worldviews, fashion statements, and addictions. As a parent, you get to watch your child spread her wings and crash. She may even come crawling back to acknowledge that you were right after all.

Everybody Needs Therapy

Psychotherapy and its handmaiden, psycho-tropic medication, are prerequisites for contemporary wellness. When children grow up without reasons to seek mental help, they find themselves to be out of step with their peers. In the last two years, almost 30 percent of American adults have either seen a mental health professional or been prescribed a drug for a mood disorder. Of those who claim they've suffered an experience warranting mental health attention, almost 40 percent have not received treatment. But the statistic most supportive of the decision to traumatize one's children is this: almost half of all adults believe their parents would have benefited from therapy.

Your Child Will Hate You

The psychological life cycle dictates that children should hate their parents. Think back on your childhood—your parents really did a number on you, right? Of course they did—it's exactly what parents are *supposed* to do. Because you love your kids, you know they deserve torture and torment. Whether you make your child suffer in exactly the same way you did or choose a new methodology, it's your responsibility to perpetuate this precious gift of intergenerational animosity.

Your Child Will Need Therapy

Those who pooh-pooh therapy tend to be so mired in denial and judgment that they don't possess the courage to explore their innermost selves. Thus it falls to those who have been traumatized to seek out this resource, because if individuals are not in enough pain, they will never willingly choose to attend the university of the inner self. Resources for the traumatized abound, from psychoanalysis to self-help groups to psychotropic medications. Those who do not believe themselves to be traumatized will never reach out to this richly arrayed support system, sentencing them to live a life that is both less aware and less colorful.

Your Child Will Be
Interesting and Creative

It's well known that most creative individuals were deeply traumatized. Your traumatized child may become a painter, musician, or graffiti artist, or might even write a memoir, the high-water mark of trauma. When your child releases a tell-all memoir about her childhood, you know you've done your job as a parent.

Your Child Will Traumatize Her Own Children

In being parented, children learn to parent. The deliberately traumatized child will grow up to be the kind of thoughtful parent you yourself want to be. When you reach the grandparenting stage of your life, you will sit on the front porch secure in the knowledge that you did your job, able to watch with pride as your grandchildren misbehave.

Overcoming Obstacles to Traumatizing Your Children

While traumatizing your children is beyond a doubt the best parenting choice, like any worthwhile endeavor, it's not necessarily easy. If you're armed with the knowledge of what to expect, however, you can anticipate problems before they become crises as well as amass the tools with which to address them.

Bumper Sticker Love

Proclaiming your parental pride on the bumper of your car (preferably a minivan or SUV) is one of the most meaningful ways to show your children how much you care. Until recently, there was little bumper sticker choice for trauma-inducing parents. Fortunately, there's a new movement afoot in bumper sticker poetry, one that celebrates the trauma we so skillfully inflict:

- My honor student fired your dumb kid.

- My kid can beat up your honor student.

- Proud parent of a stupid kid.

- My kid can let himself in the door, cook dinner, and read himself a bedtime story.

- My kid sells term papers to your honor student.

- My kid was loser of the month.

You Didn't Like the Way You Were Traumatized

Many people look back on their own childhood and critique the way their parents traumatized them. Fortunately, there is a whole range of trau-matizing techniques from which to choose. With the help of this book, you can establish your own traumatic parenting style rather than repeat that of your parents like most people. You don't have to be imprisoned by your childhood—you can be empowered by it.

Americans Are Top Traumatizers!

According to UNICEF, the United States is the second-best place in the world to traumatize children, topped only by England (those darn Brits). A 2007 study of developed countries revealed that American youths are global leaders in poor diets, excessive weight, low physical activity levels, and infrequent family dinners. The United States also set the pace for high exposure to violence and bullying, not to mention the high number of fifteen-year-olds who smoke, drink, and have sex. God bless America!

Traumatizing Your Children Is Hard Work

There's no question that parenting is the toughest job you'll ever love. Once you bring a tiny, helpless life into the world, however, you have a responsibility to traumatize that child to the best of your abilities. This takes some major planning and conviction. As you adopt your chosen traumatizing style, its approach will slowly become second nature. It may be challenging at first, but soon you'll be traumatizing your child exactly as you hoped—seemingly without effort. Your child will see how much work you've put into the process, and feel grateful that you traumatized him with such care.

Doubts About Your Chosen Traumatizing Approach

Because parenting is so challenging, there's no avoiding the fact that some days you will question all you've chosen for your child. Especially in adolescence, your child will throw everything you do in your face, questioning your values and actions. These reactions are natural and mean you're doing everything right. Maintain confidence! When it comes to trauma, there's no wrong way— there's only poor execution.

Criticism from Others

Different parenting approaches can drive wedges between the closest of friends. When one friend turns out to be an overbearing stage parent and the other is an indulgent, spineless fish, conflict is bound to arise. While it's tempting to critique the way others have chosen to parent, it's best to mind your own business and stay true to your chosen course. Unfortunately, not all parents will be as diplomatic as you. Some may criticize the traumatizing approach that you've selected. Others may actually believe it's possible to avoid trauma entirely. In a deluded effort to parent perfectly, they read books that profess to teach foolproof methods of behavior, discipline, and compassion. Unfortunately, these approaches tend to set up unrealistic expectations for a "healthy" outcome. When you encounter these naysayers, don't even try to reason with them— as a parent, your mantra should be "Never explain, never justify."

Trauma: Beneficial and Inevitable

While perhaps you've long suspected that traumatizing was the right way to parent, now you've got some tangible evidence on your side. Armed with motivation and resolve, you're on the road to being the best traumatizer you can be. In the next chapter, we'll explore some dynamics that are consistent to all traumatizing approaches so that you can mingle the basics into whatever specific style you determine is appropriate for your family.

DYNAMICS OF UNIVERSAL TRAUMA

2

BUILDING THE FOUNDATION

While parenting for maximum trauma can manifest itself in various styles, there are certain fundamentals that will scar children no matter your approach. For guidance, we need look no further than the genesis of the mental health industry. Ushered in by Sigmund Freud in the late nineteenth century, psychoanalysis had us looking inward in a manner no less revolutionary than such outward travel as journeying into space. Because much of this exploration focused on childhood development, we now have a wealth of information on exactly what traumatizes children.

The principles outlined in this book draw on decades of research and studies, performed both in the laboratory and out in the field. Parent according to these principles and you will achieve the desired results—rest assured.

> ### 💬 Tidings of Trauma
>
> *"Your responsibility as a parent is not as great as you might imagine. You need not supply the world with the next conqueror of disease or major motion-picture star. If your child simply grows up to be someone who does not use the word 'collectible' as a noun, you can consider yourself an unqualified success."*
>
> **—Fran Lebowitz**

Unreliability: The Enemy of Security and Trust

Parental unreliability is at the root of the majority of childhood trauma. It can unseat even the healthiest child's self-esteem. Unreliability erodes trust of all kinds—trust that others will care, trust that others will tell the truth, trust that others will be there when the going gets tough. Indeed, most children who grow up with unreliable parents have difficulty trusting as adults, so your unreliability will set your kids up for a lifetime of dysfunctional and failed relationships.

The most basic form of unreliability starts in early childhood—are you there when your child cries? While the indulgent parent will be there too much, not allowing the child to develop his own forms of self-soothing, and the neglectful parent will almost never be there, the most effective form of unreliability is sometimes to be there and sometimes not. Inconsistency is an integral part of traumatic parenting, and over the years inconsistent reliability will translate in your child's memory into out-and-out unreliability. Your child should never know when you will respond to his needs, when he will get a kiss on his boo-boo, when he will be told to buck up and get on with it, or, best of all, when he will be completely ignored.

As your child gets older, you can begin lying to her, proving that people can't be trusted. In accordance with your child's developmental stages, this will start with small fibs, such as the existence of Santa, the Tooth Fairy, and the Easter Bunny; escalate into larger misrepresentations, including a sex talk that points to birds, bees, cabbage patches, and storks; mature into temporal prevarication when you say "I'll be back soon" then go on a three-day bender; and peak when you inform your child, say, that the man who raised her is not, in fact, her real father. While you may feel guilty for lying (indeed, emphasis on honesty for its own sake may be one of the numbers your parents pulled on you), remember that you're fibbing for a higher goal—to damage your child's ability to trust.

Dr. Jekyll or Mr. Hyde? Fostering Unpredictability

Successfully traumatized children should never know what kind of home or situation they are walking into, and they should have no idea what kind of response their behavior will garner. One afternoon the kids should come home to find a nurturing parent who's curious about what happened at school. The next day, they should

Branding Them for Life

One of the very first acts of parenthood is choosing a name that will accompany a child throughout his life. Why pass up this opportunity to scar your child deeply and repeatedly?

If you prefer the traditional route, select a name that many of your child's peers will also have. Whether you're inspired by a book such as *Beyond Jennifer & Jason, Madison & Montana* or you surf the Internet for top rankings, an overly common name will help your child feel that he doesn't have his own identity and will assure that he must use his last initial in school.

In another direction, you can follow in the footsteps of trend-setting celebrities by inventing something unique or just plain weird, such as star-offspring monikers Pilot Inspektor, Heavenly Hiraani Tiger Lily, or Moon Unit. If you're drawn to the narcissist parenting type (see chapter 5), name your child after yourself—even multiple times, as with boxer George Foreman's five sons.

If you're uncertain how best to traumatize your child on his birth certificate, however, you can hire a child-naming consultant, newly anointed professionals who understand that *everything* today is a brand—including your child's name.

encounter a parent who's racing around the house in a manic rage, angry at them through no fault of their own, evincing no concern whatsoever for what transpired at school. Each parent's version of these scenarios will differ; the important thing to remember is that your children should never be able to guess what awaits them behind the house or car door.

Beyond your larger moods, you should never respond to your child in a predictable way. If your child gets a C+, for example, try to pitch a fit one semester, grounding him for two weeks, and the next semester let him know that you understand that he tried his best. This will nurture your child's fear of the unknown, and gradually he will start hiding things from you and declining to seek your counsel, both of which will point him in ever more problematic life directions.

Consistent Inconsistency

Nothing keeps a child on her toes like inconsistency. In a child's first years, this should manifest itself in a lack of routine. Regular mealtimes and bedtimes are anathema to the trauma-tized child—avoid them strenuously, frequently changing the protocol. Some days you'll want to bathe your child in the morning, while other times she'll get a bath right before bed. Routine is one of the surest ways to stunt your child's traumatization, so it is to be avoided at all costs.

When it comes to discipline and expectations for your child's behavior, you'll want to practice setting rules only to break them. The old saying "Do as I say, not as I do" will be your guiding principle. For example, during the teen years, you will want to forbid your child from drinking to excess while flaunting your drinking at every turn. If you hold your child to certain standards that you cannot live up to yourself, your child will become sneaky and hypocritical, knowing there is wiggle room in every standard.

There is one exception to the rule of inconsistency, however: overly rigid parenting that fails to take into account anything about the child herself will also provide trauma, generally resulting in a child who cannot think for herself.

Your Child's Cues and Needs: Ignore Them

Your parenting approach should have nothing whatsoever to do with what your child actually wants or needs. You are the parent, you know best, and your needs come first.

Throughout their lives, children will give you cues, some of them subtle and others quite overt. Your job is to second-guess those messages or, best of all, not hear them. If you do accidentally happen to receive a signal, you can either ignore it or, in an alternatively effective approach, ridicule it. For example, if your child is behaving in a needy way, the last thing you should do is reassure her. Instead, go about your own business, and if she persists in communicating her needs, make fun of her by calling attention to her immaturity.

By not listening to your children, they will develop insecurities about their worthiness and whether or not they know their own minds. They will doubt their instincts and behave as doormats in relationships. Sooner or later, they will stop

Cinematic Traumatic Parenting

When getting into the traumatizing mindset, it can be helpful to experience depictions of others who have successfully embodied the role you seek to emulate:

Controller

- *The Great Santini*
- *Mommie Dearest*
- *Black Swan*
- *The Virgin Suicides*

Pusher

- *Dead Poets Society*
- *The Turning Point*
- *Shine*

Narcissist

- *Mermaids*
- *The Squid and the Whale*
- *The Manchurian Candidate*

Indulger

- *Clueless*
- *Willy Wonka & the Chocolate Factory*

Best Friend

- *The Professional*
- *Thirteen*
- *Grey Gardens*

Self-Esteem Killer

- *Cinderella*
- *Now, Voyager*
- *Carrie*

Neglector

- *American Beauty*
- *Home Alone*
- *The Nanny Diaries*

expressing themselves entirely. Or, they could become bombastic know-it-alls out of fear that no one will listen to them as adults.

As with the rule of inconsistency, there is one exception to the principle of discounting your child's needs, and like inconsistency, that exception falls into the category of an extreme. Parents who indulge a child's every utterance, as you will see in chapter 6, will traumatize that child just as surely as if they had ignored her.

Warring Parenting Styles: 'Til Death Do You Part

For children who are lucky enough to have both parents involved in their upbringing, whether those parents are married or divorced, the most effective path to trauma lies in each parent having a different approach to child rearing.

As parents, you never want to present a united front to your children. The most common and intuitive form of this parenting technique manifests as "good cop, bad cop." When one parent is punishing a child, the other eases the pain of discipline with a treat. If one parent enforces a homework regimen, the other parent will propose a last-minute weeknight game of miniature golf. While "good cop, bad cop" is well known, it's not the only such combination. For example, one of you could be controlling while the other systematically crushes self-esteem, or one of you could be indulgent while the other pushes for a national title in figure skating. The options are endless as long as the parents make sure their efforts never duplicate or reflect one another.

The Seven Parenting Styles: Which One Suits You?

While it's critical to understand the foundational principles of traumatic child rearing, the meat of this book lies in the seven distinct parenting styles covered in the following chapters. Be sure to take the time to read through and consider each style, rather than jump ahead to the one you think may suit you best. Each has much to learn from the others, and it would not be without precedent to combine all of them into

Traumatic Intentions

For many of the most prevalent traumatizing approaches, the acceptance trend is on the upswing. According to a recent survey by market research firm Synovate, 43 percent of parents would like to be best friends with their offspring (see chapter 7, "Parent as Best Friend: We Share Everything"), and 40 percent would buy their children everything they wanted if it were within their means (see chapter 6, "Parent as Indulger: Indulgence Begets Entitlement").

This parallels an evolution in the way we view children's roles in our lives (similar to our contemporaneous shift toward parenting and spoiling our housepets). According to sociology professor Sampson Lee Blair, families used to view children as "financial assets" necessary to help out on the farm. Now, however, parents interact with their children as "emotional assets, the objects of their love and affection."

one supernova approach to traumatic parenting. You might also surprise yourself by choosing another style. Either way, at the very least, you'll have more tools in your kit for the complex, lifelong challenge that is parenting.

YOUR CHILD,
YOUR PROPERTY

PARENT AS CONTROLLER

As a controlling parent, you know what's right. You know what your child should fear and what she should believe. You have the final say in what your child should wear every day, what friends she should have, and how much food she should put in her mouth. There are so many advantages to taking complete control over your child's life. Really, what does she know? She's just a kid! It takes a bit of work to become a controlling parent, but the results for your child are most impressive—obedience, rigidity, psychosomatic stomachaches, lack of resourcefulness, and a lifetime of discontent. In terms of trauma, control is a bona fide jackpot.

Should You Be a Controller?

The controller is a special type of parent, best suited to individuals with leadership skills and a strong perfectionist drive, generally undergirded by a stimulating combination of failed dreams and entrenched self-loathing. An estimated 50 percent of controlling parents were themselves controlled by their own parents, giving a leg up to those who enjoyed this type of upbringing but far from ruling out those who did not.

The advantages to controlling your child are plentiful. You'll save yourself the inconvenience of having to deal with gray areas and your child's indecision—for example, an hour-long morning debate about the comparative merit of the pink versus the purple tights could be resolved in mere seconds with white tights, which happen to be the only ones currently available.

While it requires diligence to control to this degree, it also makes your job easier because it results in early-stage obedience. In his teen years, your child may rebel, but at that point you can send him away to "wilderness camp" or a "working ranch." Some of these "educational" opportunities even take place in other countries, allowing your child to see the world as well as permitting you to skirt pesky American laws against corporal punishment.

Controlling cross-pollinates well with a few other traumatic parenting types—the pusher, the narcissist, and the self-esteem killer—though its tools of manipulation and domination can inform all parenting approaches. The basic rule of thumb is, if it irritates you or you have an opinion on it, take control.

Tidings of Trauma

"There is no such thing as 'fun for the whole family.'"

—Jerry Seinfeld

You will gravitate toward control if you exhibit any of the following characteristics, behaviors, or beliefs, whether in parenting or in other aspects of your life, such as work or marriage:

Big Mother

Who needs the stress of keeping a watchful eye on your children? From high- to low-tech, it's never been easier with these devices:

Child safety harness: Like a leash for toddlers, this is the tried-and-true. Now these harnesses come in the form of cuddly stuffed-animal backpacks so you can strap your child in and lead her by the tail!

RFID tag: Children's clothes are now available with radio-frequency identification (RFID) tags, which are traceable within a certain radius. An alarm can be triggered if determined boundaries are breached.

Mobile location service: With GPS technology, parents can pinpoint the location of their child's phone. By programming key areas, such as school or home, parents can be notified when a child arrives at or leaves a location.

Car trackers: Numerous gadgets will now monitor a teen's driving behaviors, including excessive speed, hard braking, broken curfews, and geographical parameters. As an added bonus, parents can retaliate in real time: remotely flashing the car's lights or honking the horn until the teen behaves.

- Everything must be done exactly how you want it or you will do it yourself.

- People don't appreciate you or understand that everything you do is for their own good.

- You believe the world is a dangerous place and you can't do too much to protect your child from harm, even if that means sacrificing freedom.

- Everybody else is stupid.

You Are the Boss

From the moment your child is born, she is a generation younger than you. What does this obvious observation mean? You know better! You have spent a lifetime developing dogma and wisdom, most likely from the school of hard knocks, and by golly, your children will benefit from it. As a parent, your role is to microman-age their every move, and their goal in life is to please you and follow your orders. You did not have children in order to submit to their feeble whims. Instead, your offspring are lumps of clay to be molded in your image. They are undeniably fortunate to have you as a parent because you know everything.

Your Children Are Your Property

Not only did you give your children life, you put a roof over their heads and food in their mouths. You pay for toys, orthodontia, and the clothing you pick out for them. All of this adds up to the fact that your children belong to you, body and soul. Until they are at least eighteen and no longer accepting money and housing from you, they must accede to your rules. Remind them frequently of this fact with such statements as, "When *you* pay the bills, *you* make the rules."

When they accept your charity, starting with that baby formula they couldn't get enough of and those pacifiers they carelessly and repeatedly lost, your children relinquish all rights to self-governance, privacy, and choice. You wiped their butts—why wouldn't you read their diaries?

Dissent Is Verboten

Why? Because you said so. What more explanation is required? You are an adult, you know best and are never wrong, and children should respect their parents and accept their leadership blindly. Your children are lucky that they have you to think for them.

When your children disagree with you, tell them they are birdbrained and ungrateful. Call attention to their status as ignorant youths. Make it clear that you love them when they agree with you. Throw a tantrum or give them the silent treatment when they don't. Limits and boundaries are clear-cut and nonnegotiable—there are none for you, and many for them. Implement whatever it takes to exercise control, because once your children get the notion that dissent will be tolerated, it's game over for you.

The Motivation of Criticism

Criticism is one of the most useful tools for the controlling parent. A child with poor self-esteem

Dysfunctional Dictionary

helicopter parent: Mom or dad who hovers over children.

nanny cam: Hidden video camera with a live feed so parents can monitor their children and/or their children's babysitter from a remote location, generally via the Internet.

is much more easily managed than one who has developed confidence through praise and independent exploration of the world. He's also more likely to believe (correctly) that he couldn't survive without you.

For the controlling parent, praise only comes when a child does exactly what he is told and internalizes your guidance. In order to motivate him to act accordingly, however, you will need criticism to push him on the right track just as gutters serve to punish a poorly thrown bowling ball. Primarily your criticism will center around his intelligence, judgment, and attempts at independent thought, all of which, clearly, are stupid.

Everything Is Dangerous

Your job as a parent is to protect your child from the infinite array of perils while instilling in her the accurate belief that life is scary. People are not to be trusted, dogs foam at the mouth, germs lurk on every binky, and death is waiting to pounce. There will be no play, because play is how children get hurt. Thanks to modern technology, GPS will accompany your offspring through childhood. Curiosity is bad, all but parent-approved friendships are to be avoided, and antibacterials will be used in all household products, not to mention travel wipes.

By teaching your child about the world's dangers, you'll be inspiring the life skill of fear. What should be feared? Everything! Until your child is appropriately apprehensive, you are there to protect her.

Stages of Control

1. **In utero:** Don't submit yourself to the pain and gore of actual labor—plan a scheduled Cesarean section, whether or not it's medically

recommended, and deliver your child on the date you choose.

2. **Infant:** Put your baby on a schedule that you prefer and let him cry it out if he doesn't like it.

3. **Baby:** Eating when hungry? That's for sissies. Instead, enforce a feeding plan that works for you.

4. **Toddler:** Dictate what your child will wear, and severely punish tantrums and expressions of will.

5. **Child:** Don't allow your child to play outside or choose her own activities and friends. Plan everything, and enforce the execution of chores when your child has an invitation to do something else.

6. **Adolescent:** Your child will start asking to attend boy-girl parties and stay out late, affording you the chance to say no over and over again.

Homeschooling: Total Control

The educational gold standard in parental control is without a question homeschooling, a movement that's been around as long as there has been the option of attending school outside the home.

With homeschooling, your child will learn only what you want her to know. She won't need to experience the havoc of socialization—the only potential bully at home is you! Because the values you instill will be 100 percent yours, sexuality, drinking, and spiritual questioning will unfold according to your timetable. Finally, as a homeschooling parent, you will never have to worry about bomb scares or mass shootings.

According to the United States Department of Education, the prevalence of homeschooling has been sharply on the uptick in recent years. No surprise there!

7. **Teen:** The mother lode of control, the teen years offer the opportunity to invade privacy, mock emerging personal taste, and put your child on a diet.

8. **Young adult:** If your child wants your financial support during her college years, she'd darn well better do exactly as you say, including attending the university of your choice.

9. **Adult:** How can you keep control over an adult? Attach strings to everything—gifts, money, and your love. Make your adult children choose between you and their significant others.

Results for the Controlled Child

If you work hard to maintain absolute control over your children, there's so much to look forward to in their adulthood. Your precious offspring will be characterized by the following blessed traits:

- Rigid and uncreative.

- Self-doubting and afraid to take risks.

- Driven to perfection but never satisfied.

- Believe everybody is criticizing or finding fault in them.

- Expect others to take advantage of them, because no one is to be trusted.

- Plagued by psychosomatic ailments such as stomachaches and headaches.

- Passive-aggressive, subject to procrastination and resistance.

- Unable to attend to their own needs, instead focusing on others to their own detriment.

- Seek significant others who are controlling and possessive.

- Prone to eating disorders and addictions.

- Deep down, resent their parents but cannot individuate from them in adulthood.

From Your Loins, Under Your Control

If you are drawn to the controlling dynamic, pat yourself on the back and consider yourself fortunate—it's such a rich, diverse approach to parenting! Not only will your child have plenty of damage to repair in adulthood, you'll have the opportunity to reflect on the results of your "I said so" experiment. No one will be able to say that you didn't do it your way, and all results will be attributable to you.

While some parents will adhere to the controlling approach in its entirety, others will take bits and pieces of control while identifying more completely with the other parenting styles. Indeed, that's one of the beauties of the controlling type—it's so universally applicable! Control is most complementary with our next parenting style, the pusher, a brilliant spotlight of enforced success. Read on, and see if this may be the right blend for you!

YOUR CHILD IS AN HONOR STUDENT

4 PARENT AS PUSHER

When you look back on your own childhood, just think of how many opportunities to mold you into a superstar were wasted! Most likely your parents didn't realize that they needed to start much earlier to shape you into a world-class ice skater, gymnast, golfer, beauty contestant, pianist, or Harvard student. If they had, who knows what your life would be like now? Fortunately, as a parent yourself, you can live those experiences vicariously as well as give your children the opportunities you never had, all the while basking in the reflected glow of your trophy children's successes.

If you're drawn to pusher parenting, you've got so much to look forward to. From as early as three years old, your child will function as a little professional with you as his manager. Your child will be the blank slate for everything you've ever dreamed about and failed to attain. By pushing your child in everything from sports to music to grades, you are doing him a huge favor, preparing him for a life of success—whether he wants it or not!

By the time your child rebels against you and descends into drug addiction and stalled motivation, you will already have several gold medals and trophies in hand to prove that it's not your fault. While it's certainly no walk in the park to carpool, fund, and push your child's way to excellence, the results are well worth it.

Should You Be a Pusher?

Parents who excel at pushing are often aficionados of public perception. If you always buy the best, care deeply what others think, and enjoy keeping up with the Joneses, you just might have what it takes to be a pusher.

Pushers believe that children are engineering projects to be subjected to the same efforts one might apply in the workplace. Guided by office tools—calendars, clipboards, spreadsheets—pushers' children's lives bear witness to the complexity of the contemporary age. If your child doesn't distinguish herself, what hope does she have of a successful adulthood?

If you are demanding and perfectionistic, you probably have natural pushing inclinations. For example, one current trend in pushing consists of women who choose to stay at home with their children following high-powered careers. These mothers apply to their children the same talents that got them ahead at work, from tracking milestones to networking to climbing the playground ladder.

Pushing blends nicely with a few other parenting styles, notably the controller, the narcissist, the indulger, and the self-esteem killer, so if you are an aspiring pusher, pay close attention to those types in order to forge your own unique approach.

You will gravitate toward pushing if you exhibit any of the following characteristics, behaviors, or beliefs, whether in parenting or in other aspects of your life, such as work or marriage:

- What others think of you determines what you think of yourself.

- You sacrifice yourself and work hard toward a higher goal, but that higher goal darn well better come through for you or your efforts will have been wasted.

- Everybody else is the competition.

- There are two types of people in this world: winners and losers.

Train Now: Childhood Is for Sissies

It used to be that childhood unfolded with little structure. Pre-adults made their way home from school with no extracurricular activities; played whatever games they chose, with whomever they choose, and suffered through long, unplanned summers. Children even got themselves from point A to point B on such mortally dangerous transportation devices as bicycles. It's a wonder anybody from those generations achieved anything at all, let alone survived!

Tidings of Trauma

"No matter how calmly you try to referee, parenting will eventually produce bizarre behavior, and I'm not talking about the kids."
—**Bill Cosby**

Fortunately, today there's a better way. Now you can plan every second of your child's time to prepare him for real life. We don't get to choose our activities at work, so we would be doing our children a disservice if we were to allow them to chase butterflies and ponder their own imaginations. You'll have no shortage of activities to choose from, thanks to the industries that have developed to improve childhood: tutoring services, Little League, youth soccer, ice-skating coaching, and instruction in such areas as art, music, ballet, and martial arts.

Not to mention that all worthwhile endeavors must start young if your child is to have any chance of world-class performance. No award-winning pianist ever started lessons as an adult. Gymnastics is over and done with by one's eighteenth birthday. And Tiger Woods achieved his first hole-in-one at the age of six. As you'll see below, academic success starts even before the child is born, with in utero applications to the right preschool, leading to the right elementary school, leading to Harvard.

Some parents worry needlessly over whether their children actually enjoy their many activities. Who cares? You know best for your child, and if she has any free time in her schedule, you're not doing a good enough job.

Perfection Is the Goal: Setting Your Child Up for Failure

For the pusher, there's no such thing as good enough—there is only perfection. If your child believes it's acceptable to shoot for mediocrity, he'll never live up to his own potential. Because there is always room to do better, the unattainability of perfection and the inevitability of failure will continually motivate your child to do more.

There are numerous antiquated adages that promote middle-of-the-road achievement, focusing on teamwork, doing one's personal best, being a good sport, and learning as you go along. These types of values are the devil's work! In order for your child to get ahead in life, it's critical that you let him know that winning and perfection should be pursued at any cost.

My Child Is an Honor Student: Where's the Plus on that A?

We live in a scholar-eat-scholar world. Your precious child is up against junior Einsteins and baby brain surgeons. By the time your child hits kindergarten, if she's not reading at a fifth-grade level, it's all over for her. As you no doubt know, academic success is now the caste system of contemporary America. If you don't get into the right preschool, with its waiting list longer than your matriculating child's life, you can kiss Harvard goodbye, because one institution feeds right into the next.

Your child should be doing at least an hour of homework daily for each successive grade. Yes, that means she'll be doing 12 hours of home-work a day by her senior year of high school, but no one ever promised academic achievement would be easy.

Some parents are tempted to look at their child's roster of A- grades as "good enough." They don't realize that an A- is the gateway to failure. Soon it'll be a B+, and before you know it, your child will be at a community college planning her "career" in data entry. How will that reflect on you?

Love Is for Winners: Your Child Is His Achievements

If your child believes you will love him no matter what, even if he's a failure, you're doing some-thing wrong. To teach your child that he has intrinsic worth whether or not he succeeds is to prepare him for an idealized world that does not exist. We *are* our successes and our failures—after all, what else is there? As a parent, you need to train your child to live on his own, and if you

Academic Doping

Why should you settle for your child's 3.8 GPA? Once solely the domain of adult bodybuilders and truck drivers, performance-enhancing drugs have finally become available for kids. Parents are now manipulating doctors into prescribing ADHD medications such as Ritalin and Adderall to help their children focus on their schoolwork.

According to a 2006 study, two-thirds of physicians reported fielding such requests to the tune of approximately 11 parents per year, and almost 10 percent of the doctors complied. When the physicians deny the requests, they estimate that 16 percent of the parents go on to obtain the drugs without medical approval. With such minor side effects as loss of appetite, irritability, blurry vision, stunted growth, hallucinations, psychotic behavior, and tics and tremors, who wouldn't go the extra distance for their child's success?

Go Team!

If your child is an athlete, you can avail yourself of many techniques to assure her wins. Between 2000 and 2003, Frenchman Christophe Fauviau, a true pusher dad, drugged the water bottles of twenty-seven opponents of his tennis-playing teenage son and daughter. Unknowingly sedated by the anti-anxiety drug Temesta, the players (one as young as eleven years old) became weak and nauseous, ensuring victory for Fauviau's children. The last incident resulted in the death of a player who, on the way home from a match, fell asleep at the wheel and crashed into a tree.

Other types of athletes also have impassioned parents behind them. A Massachusetts hockey dad fatally punched another father in the head during his son's scrimmage. The state of Texas is quite the hotspot for pusher parents: in 2005, a disgruntled father shot his son's football coach, and in 1991, a cheerleading mom hired a hit man to take out her daughter's rival's mother so the daughter would not be able to compete.

The best aspect of this type of athletic parenting is that children don't even have to be very good players. Fauviau's son, for example, was by all accounts mediocre with the racket, playing matches for purses as small as $50.

coddle him with love that he didn't earn, he'll be helpless and lazy once he strikes out on his own. Performance equals love—don't let him think anything different.

Public Acclaim Above All

Performance is the public exhibition of skill, talent, and practice. The answer to the old philosophical question "If a tree falls in the forest and nobody is there to hear it, does it make a sound?" is absolutely not. Why would you spend all those hours in training only to hide your achievements away from the public eye? Our culture is full of reasons to perform, from *Dirty Dancing*'s "Nobody puts Baby in a corner" to the song lyrics "This little light of mine / I'm gonna let it shine."

Your children should grow up knowing that externally validated success means everything. Internal fulfillment is a luxury most of us can't afford. When you *are* your achievements, the world will sit up and take notice.

Stages of Pushing

1. **In utero:** Play classical music for the fetus by putting Bose headphones on the pregnant belly. Map out your child's future. Apply to preschools.

2. **Infant:** Play books on tape in foreign languages while your infant naps.

3. **Baby:** Teach sign language so your baby can communicate before the speech area of her brain develops.

4. **Toddler:** Put golf clubs, violins, or picture-free books in your child's hands. Call your child "little man" or "little lady" and react to childish behavior with ridicule.

5. **Child:** Expose your child to a wide range of activities until no minute is unscheduled, or focus your child on only one activity so that he might become world-class.

6. **Adolescent:** Argue with teachers and coaches who want to hold your child back. Hire tutors and begin prepping for the SATs.

7. **Teen:** Consult a college counselor and choose a target school by age fourteen. Plot out all the extracurriculars, grades, and advanced-placement courses it will take to get there.

8. **Young adult:** Have your child's college grades sent to your home. If your child did not get into a top school, explore transfer possibilities.

9. **Adult:** Hold your child to a rite-of-passage schedule that reflects well on you among your friends: marriage, childbirth, and professional advancement.

Results for the Pushed Child

By pushing your children to achieve perfection, you'll mold adults characterized by the following superstar traits:

• Inflexible, risk averse, unplayful, uncreative.

- Never satisfied with accomplishments, never good enough, never feel like they measure up.

- Prone to anxiety, depression, and psychosomatic complaints.

Dysfunctional Dictionary

hurried-child syndrome: Condition in which parents overschedule their children's lives, push them hard for academic success, and expect them to behave and react as miniature adults.

hyper-parenting: Child-rearing style characterized by intense parental involvement in managing, scheduling, and enriching all aspects of their children's lives.

trophy child: Child used to impress other people and enhance parental status.

- Unsuccessful at directing and negotiating their own lives after so much structure.

- Likely to bow out of pursuits they once worked so hard to master.

- Resentful of their parents.

- Struggles with addiction.

- Anger issues.

Push Them Now,
Before It's Too Late

Your children are only with you for a short time, so make the most of it. With all that you've sacrificed to give them every advantage, they should reflect well on you and reaffirm the choice you've made to put them first. If they protest, remember that it's just the shortsighted voice of a child speaking. You know that the long-term rewards will be worth so much more than any short-term discomfort.

Next we'll explore a parenting style that shares some characteristics with the pusher: the parental narcissist. What do you want to see when you look in the mirror of your child's face? Yourself!

IT'S ALL
ABOUT YOU

PARENT AS NARCISSIST

Narcissism is very hip, very hot, very now. Once upon a time, people cared about the community and the world they lived in. Now, however, families more frequently put themselves above the good of the group. It doesn't matter if someone else's Johnny fails school—all they care about is their Joey. Some skilled parents, however, take this typology to a new, individualized level of advancement by actually putting *themselves* ahead of their own children.

Narcissism is the one dynamic that runs through all of the parenting types. The controlling parent, for example, is most certainly blessed with a strong dose of narcissism, as are the pusher and the best friend.

In its purest form, however, the glory of narcissism manifests itself as relating everything back to oneself, governed by the true inability to put anybody else's interests first. As you can imagine, this lack of reciprocity makes for a truly fascinating childhood.

Grabbing the Medical Spotlight

Because children are attention seekers, they frequently pull focus from their parents. One solution to this problem is Munchausen Syndrome by Proxy (MSbP), whereby a parent induces illness in a child in order to receive sympathy from others. In the Eminem song "Cleanin' Out My Closet," for example, the rapper states, "Goin' through public housing systems, victim of Munchausen Syndrome / My whole life I was made to believe I was sick when I wasn't." While some experts dispute the validity of MSbP, there is plenty of anecdotal evidence to support its utility as a narcissistic parenting technique.

Should You Be a Narcissist?

Narcissistic parents enjoy one of the broadest arenas of traumatic impact because they don't put their children's needs first. As an aspiring narcissist, you should be proud to note that such dynamics infuse all of the other parenting types— indeed, narcissistic parenting takes the traumatic-parenting crown, so if you find yourself in this category, congratulate yourself on your choice!

Narcissistic parents refer all outside events to themselves, interpreting a child's behavior as having been intended to reject, insult, or harm them in some way. Prior to having children, narcissists have experienced this phenomenon in other areas—being underappreciated, perceiving others' envy, fielding accusations that they are exploitative, and flying into narcissistic rages. It may have been challenging to conduct mature relationships, with existing interactions characterized by excessive dependence and manipulation.

Fortunately, children adore their parents, so your need for acclaim will be endlessly satisfied once you've reproduced. Parental narcissism is one of the best ways to get the kudos you so deserve!

You will gravitate toward narcissism if you exhibit any of the following characteristics, behaviors, or beliefs, whether in parenting or in other aspects of your life, such as work or marriage:

- You fantasize about omnipotence.

- You love being the center of attention.

- You find it difficult to understand why others struggle with their petty problems.

- Deep down (unacknowledged to others, of course), you feel defective.

Children Were Born to Love Their Parents

Children have no inherent value other than what they can do for you. Think about all you've sacrificed for them—the sex you had in order to conceive them, pregnancy and delivery, financial outlays, the fact that they interrupt you all the time. You've done your job and met your end of the bargain. Everything else is up to them.

You *deserve* their love. What child doesn't adore and respect his parents? It's the law of the universe, and if you don't see that filial worship in his eyes, then he's darn well going to feel what it's like to live without his parents' affection. Because you're a superhero to him, your child must express his love for you with praise—for your personality, your perfume, your outfits, your sex appeal. You gave your child life—now he must learn to meet your ever-shifting emotional needs.

Shut Up! Squelch that Voice

Children are meant to be neither seen nor heard—except when it's convenient or when they're caring for you, reflecting well on you, or boosting your ego in some way. Your child has very little to say about the world—after all, she's just a child! How interesting could she be? Instead, she should be basking in the fascination of your stories and experiences. Indeed, it's vital that you turn every conversation back to yourself. If she's had a bad day at school, tell her "That's nothing. When I was your age . . ." She should sympathize with you—not the other way around.

If your child has an interest or concern that you don't share, ignore her until she returns to a topic that you enjoy. (Indifference is a powerful tool for guiding your children without them knowing it.) The general rule of thumb is that her interests and hobbies are silly and stupid, but yours are fascinating and worthwhile. Over time, she'll come to agree.

Your Needs Come First

Children like to be the center of attention, but this draws the spotlight away from you. Your child should never be better looking, smarter, or more successful than you. The moment they begin to shine in a way that threatens your stardom, shoot them down. For example, when you play sports or cards, play to win, even if it involves cheating. Anything they can do, you can do better.

Dysfunctional Dictionary

birth art: Art that depicts or celebrates one's pregnancy or childbirth, including the *belly cast,* a plaster cast of a pregnant woman's stomach that is often used to make a highly adorned sculpture for display in the home.

brag book: Small, portable photo album to show strangers, especially on airplanes and at book clubs.

gallery wall: Mass display of family photographs, often professionally taken, that remind parents of the beautiful family they've created.

holiday newsletter: Annual letter that boasts about the achievements of one's offspring, generally highly exaggerated so as to reflect well on the parents and make recipients feel inferior.

When you are in a bad mood or have a headache, your children must not only keep their needs to themselves, they should take care of you. This is especially important if you make the parenting choice to be an alcoholic or other type of addict, as you will require plenty of care, and who better to give it than your kids?

If your children fail to recognize the value of your needs, you'll want to remind them how important you are by bragging about yourself or by teasing or embarrassing them. Soon enough they'll fall in line!

> ### 💬 Tidings of Trauma
>
> *"The first half of our life is ruined by our parents and the second half by our children."*
> —*Clarence Darrow*

Counter with Contempt

Your children should never forget that your love is conditional. After all, what value would love have if it were guaranteed? If your child toes the line, you will reward him with seductive, charming behavior. If your child expresses himself and contradicts you, the gloves come off! No child should ever criticize a parent, especially you, and you will not allow such sacrilege. Overall, your child must understand that he is not to have his own feelings—yours are the only ones that matter.

To punish any form of boat rocking, you have numerous tools at your disposal. You can show them how much they've hurt you and play the guilt card, you can throw a tantrum and intimidate them, or you can employ the silent treatment and withhold your love and affection. Finally, you can threaten to abandon your child, a remarkably effective tactic.

Stages of Narcissistic Parenting

1. **In utero:** Having a baby is all about the shower, the gifts, the cute little shoes, and choosing an appropriately weird (extra points for creative spelling!) name. Or, you may want to name your child after yourself.

2. **Infant:** People will continue to give you lots of attention for having a newborn. When you send out baby announcements, make sure that you pat yourself on the back for managing to procreate.

3. **Baby:** When your baby cries or expresses needs, just walk away. How annoying!

The Mesmerizing Mirror

Many narcissists fail to recognize their noble tradition and its etymology. The term stems from the Greek myth of Narcissus, the son of a god and a nymph, who was renowned for his extreme physical beauty. Though there are a few different renditions of the myth, in the generally accepted version, Narcissus angers the gods by rejecting a romantic interest. As punishment, Narcissus is made to fall in love with his own reflection in the waters of a spring, gazing at himself until he dies. Upon his death, the sweet-smelling flower that bears his name grows in his spot by the waters, drooping its head just as he bowed to see his reflection.

While the story has anti-narcissistic roots, serving as a morality tale warning against self-love, this message is now antiquated. Since the original incident in ancient Greece, no one has died from gazing at themselves in the mirror, except perhaps while driving. Instead, it's useful to understand the story for its psychoanalytic meaning—an ample degree of self-involvement and self-reference. From this perspective, child-rearing can only enhance a parent's life, because children are the ultimate self-reference and function beautifully to reflect the narcissist.

4. **Toddler:** Dress your child exactly like you, then yell if she spills on her outfit. Lock your bedroom door so your child can't disturb you if she has a nightmare.

5. **Child:** Finally—your child can get you beer from the fridge and actually pitch in around the house.

6. **Adolescent:** Punish only those behaviors that irritate you, paying no attention to those that are actually bad for her.

7. **Teen:** Remove her bedroom door from its hinges—privacy is for you and you alone!

8. **Young adult:** Leave repeated phone messages calling her ungrateful and mean. Cry. When something happens in her world, make sure she knows it's worse for you.

9. **Adult:** Leave repeated phone messages calling her ungrateful and mean. Cry. When something happens in her world, make sure she knows it's worse for you.

Results for the Narcissistically Parented Child

If you work hard to make sure your children know it's all about you, there's so much to look forward to in their adulthood. Your ungrateful offspring will be characterized by the following useful traits:

- Seek acceptance from others, at their own expense.

- Will often enter into relationships with narcissists. (May even become narcissists themselves!)

- Under- or overdeveloped boundaries.

- Strong tendencies toward codependence.

- "Mama's boys" and "Daddy's girls."

- Unsure of their own feelings and emotions; often unable to identify or modulate them.

- Dampened sense of self.

- Drug and alcohol addiction.

- Avoid you in adulthood, possibly changing their phone numbers and moving far away.

Your Child, Your Mirror

Thank goodness you had children—they are your legacy, your genetically superior yes-men, your support system not only for old age, but for *whole* age! Yes, they're bound to let you down, but with a few strokes of manipulation, you'll have them right back where you want them—until they leave for good. For narcissists, because it's hard to maintain successful relationships, it's necessary to birth them.

Next we'll explore a parenting style that, despite appearances, has much in common with the narcissist. It also involves buying or bribing your child's love. Read on as we explore the indulger!

INDULGENCE BEGETS ENTITLEMENT

6 PARENT AS INDULGER

You didn't have a child to deny her or set limits.
After all, she'll only be with you for eighteen
years—though it's bound to be at least ten more,
given how much she enjoys being indulged—so
why spend it saying no? Discipline will wear you
both down, with endless battles about homework,
talking back, and manners. Why not just avoid
the whole thing? Your child will *want* to behave
because you're going to give her everything you
didn't have. No pair of jeans is too expensive, even
if she's still growing. When she gets into trouble,
you're going to do your best to get her out of
it without accountability or apology. She's your
little angel—how dare they say otherwise?

Once you commit to raising a little prince or princess who will grow up to be an entitled, boredom-stricken, unresourceful brat, you've got a fail-safe parenting path for every childhood phase. While this approach can be more expensive than others and often entails sharing your bed with your children, there are many worthwhile rewards!

Should You Be an Indulger?

Indulgent parents are a special breed. Many waited until they were older and better established in their own lives to start their families. With their higher income bracket, work challenges, and a belief that they can execute perfect child rearing merely by reading books and paying for private schools, indulgence comes naturally to these parents. Indeed, the indulger type frequently overlaps with the neglector, since some use indulgence to compensate for spending so much time away from their children. Some indulgent parents experienced poverty in their youth, so they're proud to be able to give to their children, while others attempt to counter their strict upbringings with an atmosphere of permissiveness. Of course,

indulgence is not just limited to material posses-
sions. It can be executed successfully when
exclusively applied to the behavioral arena as well.

While parenting approaches like control and
pushing take conscious work, indulgence is just
the opposite—it's easy! You don't have to teach
your children manners, morals, or a work ethic,
and you avoid the unpleasantness that comes
with saying no. Finally, you make it more likely
that your child will like you all the time, and
what could be better than that?

Dysfunctional Dictionary

kidfluence: Impact children have on their
parents' purchasing decisions.

nag factor: Degree to which parents' purchasing decisions are based on their children's
repetitive demands.

pester power: Children's ability to persuade
parents to purchase items they would not
otherwise buy or perform actions they would
not otherwise do.

You will gravitate toward indulgence if you exhibit any of the following characteristics, behaviors, or beliefs, whether in parenting or in other aspects of your life, such as work or marriage:

- You're lazy.

- You believe that whatever will be will be, and your job is only to watch fate unfold.

> ### Tidings of Trauma
>
> *"The thing that impresses me most about America is the way parents obey their children."*
> **—Edward, Duke of Windsor**

- You had kids because you came up with some great ideas for decorating the nursery.

- Only other people's children behave poorly (which, of course, is attributable to poor parenting).

Your Child Is the Center of the Universe

Your child's birth was the second coming, and everything stopped so you could create the perfect world for him. Every peep and poop was sacred. When it came time for feedings and sleeping, you let him set the schedule—after all, who better knows what he needs than the infant himself?

Your job as a parent is to teach your child that the world revolves around him. To do this, always make your child's wishes the top priority. There's no such thing as give and take—for your child, there is only take, whenever he wants. If you have friends over for dinner, for example, and your child interrupts an interesting discussion, don't tell him to wait because someone else is speaking. Instead, stop everything and pay attention to your child. It's okay to make your friends feel like interlopers.

Sacrifice your marriage to your child if necessary. If your child prefers that you stay home and throws a tantrum when you plan a date night, cancel your dinner reservations and stay home. Your child should not comprehend that sometimes it's necessary to wait or that other people have pesky needs and desires—if he does, you're not doing your job.

No Limits, No Boundaries

Discipline is for mean, evil parents—not to mention that discipline is the least fun part of the parent's job! Your child will tell you when she wants to go to bed, when she wants to eat broccoli, when she wants to do schoolwork. If you're the kind of person who buys organic fruit and uses canvas grocery bags, you can justify your parenting approach as "natural."

The indulgent parent lets the child be in charge. Always give in to your child's tantrums. If her lower lip so much as quivers, give her what she wants. Your child should never suffer through a crying spell that lasts longer than a few seconds. On the rare occasion that you do create a rule, always be prepared to negotiate it, especially with young children, and ultimately give in. Your children will test you constantly, and you want to show them that it works.

Never Hold Your Child Accountable

It is *never* your child's fault. When your child attempts to blame someone else for a problem, encourage this resourceful response. If your child gets into trouble, whether in school, with friends, or with the law, always do whatever you can to bail him out. Nobody but you is allowed to discipline your child, and even you don't do it! You must protect your child from this type of persecution. How dare they?

While many parents believe in assigning chores so children will learn to work hard and contribute to the family, the indulger knows that this battle isn't worth fighting, not to mention that many indulgers have housekeepers. Since your child will probably grow up to be a model, actor, professional athlete, or celebrity personal assistant, what does he need a work ethic for?

Overpraise Your Child

Your child is a beautiful, handsome, charming genius, and your job is to boost her self-esteem sky-high. Never withhold praise from your child, even if she's doing something you'd prefer that she not do. For example, if she's running all over the house like a dervish, breaking lamps and scuffing floors, praise her lightning-quick speed!

If your child is involved in an activity that requires multiple steps, praise every step of the performance rather than solely applauding the final result. This way your child will come to expect credit for even the most minor of accomplishments. Praise should be the carrot that motivates your child, rather than the intrinsic reward of a job well done.

Undeserved, unlimited praise is one of the best ways for a parent to instill a deep sense of entitlement. When your child grows up and goes out into the world, you'll know you've done your job when she can't understand why nobody else likes her.

Start 'Em Young

Doesn't your child deserve luxury goods? Fortunately, recent years have seen a rise in items that aren't just good enough for your offspring— they're good enough for you!

Ferrari Testarossa two-seater car for kids: $97,395. Available in black, blue, pink, red, white, and yellow; price does not include optional stereo system and seatbelts.

Maclaren GB Type-Au stroller: Over $3,000. Limited edition. Black leather upholstery. Comes with 9-karat gold crest that can be detached and worn as brooch.

Goyard diaper bag: About $3,000. Made to order to match your luggage set.

Fantasy Coach bed: $47,000. Just like the pre-pumpkin Cinderella model.

Baby Dior cotton christening dress: $1,335. Matching hat available for $138.

Tumble Outpost: $122,730. Backyard play structure. Price includes twelve-foot super slide, but not assembly or bark chips.

Custom Couture fashion design kit: $895. Kit provides materials for child to design a garment, which is then created as a one-of-a-kind outfit.

Buy Your Child's Love

Children are becoming consumers at younger and younger ages, thanks to clever advertising campaigns that are targeted directly at your offspring. No longer is it the parents' job to introduce kids to products and materialism—if you let your child sit in front of the television for a few hours a day, he'll know what he wants soon enough. He will make his taste clear when you go to the market, toy store, and mall by begging you to finance the objects of his desire.

Some parents force their children to work for their money, saving up to buy their desired non-essentials. To the indulger, this is just plain crass. Putting your child to work, as if he were household staff? The "meaning of money," which such slave driver parents quote as a lesson for their children, is that it grows on plastic trees.

Instead, you want to buy your child whatever he wants, charging it if you must. Pay no attention to whether your child craves toys that he will quickly tire of, or whether the clothing he wants is age-inappropriate. If he wants it, get it! Your job is to make sure he is never bored or insecure in comparison with his friends. Remember how important designer jeans were in your youth? *Never* allow your child to suffer the anguish of going without.

By buying your child whatever he wants, he will love you more. You'll be able to direct his behavior with bribes, and he'll learn that he must behave to receive presents. Save up a list of things you know he wants so that when you need him to do something he doesn't feel like doing, you can dangle one of them as an incentive. Because your child has the best toys, clothes, and food, other children will want to play at your house. Kids like stuff, and they like doing what they want to do. As an indulger parent, your kids will like you all the time!

Stages of Indulgence

1. **In utero:** Decorate the nursery with stuffed animals and toys your child will not need for years. Buy multiple cute outfits for your child to grow into.

2. **Infant:** Don't put your child on any kind of sleep or eating schedule.

3. **Baby:** Whenever your child cries, pick her up.

4. **Toddler:** If your toddler has a tantrum, give her whatever she wants. Rather than asking her to help you pick up her toys, clean up after her. No bedtime.

5. **Child:** Take your child to malls and toy stores and let her have whatever she wants. If she wants you to stay home with her when you have plans, cancel your plans. No bedtime.

Tidings of Trauma

"All I've got at home is two dogs and four cats and six bunny rabbits and two parakeets and three canaries and a green parrot and a turtle and a bowl of goldfish and a cage of white mice and a silly old hamster! I want a squirrel!"
—Veruca Salt, in Roald Dahl's
Charlie and the Chocolate Factory

6. **Adolescent:** Allow your child to attend concerts and stay out late. Don't put any limits on TV or video game time. If her grades suffer, bribe her with clothing or electronics, or just let the grades slip.

7. **Teen:** Your child will probably not want to participate in any family activities, such as dinner or gatherings. Let her do whatever she wants, and don't enforce any kind of curfew.

8. **Young adult:** Whenever your child gets into trouble, bail her out. Give her money whenever she requests it.

9. **Adult:** Don't ask your child to move out at any age. Send her money whenever she requests it.

Results for the Indulged Child

If you put effort toward indulging your child's every whim, there's so much to look forward to in adulthood. Your gourmet offspring will be characterized by the following entitled traits:

- Chronic boredom thanks to never having learned to entertain themselves.

- Low tolerance for frustration.

- Demanding and self-centered.

- Face a harsh reality when they get into outside world without parents to pave the way.

- Bosses will hate them because they think they're special without having to work for anything.

- Believe rules don't apply to them.

- Don't respect other people's rights.

- Try to control people; manipulative.

- Don't know the difference between needs and wants.

- Poor money-management skills.

- Whiners.

- Dependent on parents into adulthood.

The Happily Spoiled Child

Your child never wants to hear you say no, and you really don't want to say it. Make both of you happy by pulling it from your vocabulary! You and your child are only on this earth for a short time, and you can't take it with you. Don't both of you deserve the best and the easiest?

Next we're going to have a look at a parenting type that dovetails nicely with the indulger—in fact, if you were to cross narcissism with indulgence, you just might get the best friend!

WE SHARE EVERYTHING

7
PARENT AS BEST FRIEND

Ah, the best-friend parent. All social woes pre-childbirth—lack of popularity, difficulty forging close adult relationships, problematic marriages—are solved for the best-friend parent after the children come along. "Mini-me" is too flat a phrase to describe these junior companions—they are confidantes and shoulders to lean on, compatriots in fun and partners in crime. There are no boundaries between the best-friend parent and her child, who go everywhere together and share everything. Whether it's dancing to the same music or smoking from the same joint, the best-friend parent and her precocious offspring exemplify togetherness.

Should You Be a Best Friend?

Does much of your identity derive from perceiving yourself as fun, hip, and young at heart? Do you love the idea of having a constant companion who's dependent on you for affection and support? If so, you may be an ideal candidate for the best-friend parent.

Best-friend parents tend to cluster in a few categories. Some didn't enjoy their own social lives as children and teens, and revel in the opportunity to reinvent themselves through their own children, while others look upon their own youths as glory days and try to stay in that headspace for as long as possible. Some think of themselves as hip despite their advanced years and feel they can stay that way by relating to their kids, thus reversing their own experience of fuddy-duddy parents. Many didn't enjoy their distanced relationships with their parents and vow not to repeat that mistake.

Best-friend parents value honesty above all else. No information should be filtered just because a child is, well, a child—instead, they're pre-adults who are going to discover the harsh truth anyway, so why not hear it from their parents? Those suited to the best-friend role think very highly of their own children and assess them as peers, professing pride in their kids' being "mature for their age"—after all, they made them that way!

Tidings of Trauma

"My mother had a great deal of trouble with me, but I think she enjoyed it."

—Mark Twain

You will gravitate toward best-friend parenting if you exhibit any of the following characteristics, behaviors, or beliefs, whether in parenting or in other aspects of your life, such as work or marriage:

- In other relationships, you've been accused of being clingy or needy, with your identity becoming submerged.

- When you're walking around downtown or at the mall, you more frequently admire what the kids are wearing than the outfits sported by people your age.

- You are relieved at the prospect of no longer having to manage your own social life.

- You really, really, really want your kids to like you.

Share Everything with Your Child

The mantra of the best-friend parent is "no boundaries." When you have a child, you've bred a confidante. It's so important that you be able to share everything with your best friend, a relationship that could suffer were you to keep any secrets. Whether the topic is finances or sex, be as explicit as possible with your child—preferably while sharing a glass of Chardonnay.

The more you discuss adult issues with your child, the more he will become adept at navigating them with you. Soon enough he'll be giving you marital advice, if you're married, or commiserating with you over the problems of your ex, if you're no longer together.

Take your child everywhere with you. Even if wedding invitations state "No Children," assume they were referring to all the *other* children, not your precious little one. If you've got poker night, bring the kid. If you're off to the nail salon, make sure she gets her fingers and toes painted too. Even strip clubs are more fun when the kids come along.

Given that you like to stay out late, your child won't need a bedtime. Not only will you save money on babysitters, everybody at the bar will comment on how cute your child is—just like a little grown-up!

Allow Your Other Relationships to Suffer

When you entered your marriage (if indeed you started your family that way), you probably had the romantic notion that wedded bliss would meet all your needs—until you had your first child. No relationship you'd experienced until then could match this new bond, and suddenly your spouse seemed so inadequate. This is a great start to a best-friend bond with your kids. Don't fall prey to such divisive elements as "date night" with your spouse, or marital counseling. Let the chips fall where they may, and hopefully at some point the spouse will be out of the picture so that you and the kids can discuss what a problem he or she was. Obviously, whether or not you stay married, your child will always take your side.

While you may have had a thriving social life before your children were born, after their arrival, don't put any effort into keeping up with your friends. This will probably happen naturally if you insist on bringing your children with you wherever you go. When your kids are older, you'll be hanging out with their friends, anyway.

Let Your Children Know You're Dependent on Them

Now that there's no competition for your affection, you'll be entirely dependent on your children for social sustenance. Make sure they know this. When you relate to your child as a surrogate spouse, using her to fill in the emptiness you feel, make sure she knows she's deserting you if she wants to do something without you. Ask if you can join, and if not, break down into tears and say, "But you're the only one who loves me!" Let them know that eventually they will have to support you, and mention how happy you will be when they give you grandchildren you can be friends with someday.

Join Your Child's Trends

Your child will keep you young! As a parent, you're fortunate that you've got a living, breathing trend-spotter coming home to you every day. All you have to do is observe and plan lots of shopping trips together. If your child wears her thong way above the waistband of her jeans, so should you! If your child wants a tattoo, get ones that match! Share music with your child so you can rock out together. When your child shares the latest slang with you, remember to incorporate it into your speech. Nothing's better than a fifty-year-old who says "dude."

Overall, your goal is to become such a buddy that you lose your parental authority, which functions as a final frontier separating you from your best-friend child. One thing that is sure to help obliterate this dysfunctional barrier is partying with your child. Not only is it safer for your child to experiment with alcohol and drugs with you rather than out on the streets, it's more fun for you! Between the two of you, your kid probably has better access to dealers than you do, and you've got that over-twenty-one driver's license—what a team!

I've Got Your Back

Baseball games are celebrated as occasions for male bonding, a place where the parental relationship can be infused with friendship. Chicago White Sox fan William Ligue Jr., for example, took offense at the Kansas City Royals first-base coach, so he and his fifteen-year-old son (both shirtless) jumped down from the stands to attack him. Following this special father-son moment, Ligue stated: "I just want to thank God for giving me the courage to do this with my son tonight. Thanks, Lord, I owe you one."

Punish Your Child Only for Being a Bad Friend

As a parent, you've got to pick and choose your battles, and the ones to avoid are those that may compromise the possibility of your children liking you. Just as you wouldn't boss around a peer, best-friend parents don't give rules or tell their children what to do.

The exception to this hands-off approach to parenting, however, is when your child behaves like a bad friend—not inviting you to a party, leaving you in the lurch on a Saturday night, neglecting to tell you an important secret, failing to wash your jeans after he's borrowed them. In these instances, crack down hard with the silent treatment, and sooner or later he'll realize what it takes to be a good friend.

Stages of Best-Friend Parenting

1. **In utero:** Start buying paraphernalia for all the things you'd like to do with your child, like a baseball mitt.

2. **Infant:** Call your child "little buddy." Start talking to your child about your feelings, even though she can't understand what you're saying.

3. **Baby:** Make sure your child still sleeps in your bed, at least through toddlerhood. Whenever your child cries, run to her, saying "I'll never leave you!"

4. **Toddler:** Buy identical outfits for yourself and your child to wear. Decline to enroll your child in preschool—that would be too much time away from you!

5. **Child:** Now that your child is ambulatory and verbal, you truly can do everything together. Take your child out of school some days just so the two of you can do fun stuff!

6. **Adolescent:** Get to know your child's friends. When she has sleepovers, stay up late with the gang and get them to confide in you about things they'd never tell their own parents. Do whatever it takes to be seen as the "fun one."

7. **Teen:** Introduce your child to drinking and drugs, if that's what you enjoy doing, or at the very least, condone it because it's cool!

8. **Young adult:** Resent the fact that your child may be striking out on her own, and stage mini-breakdowns to bring her back to your side.

9. **Adult:** Do whatever you can to make your child move back in with you and tell her that neither of you needs anybody else.

Dysfunctional Dictionary

askable parent: Parent who encourages and is willing to answer questions about sex and other adult topics.

MILF: From "*mother I'd like to fuck,*" a term characterizing sexually appealing mothers (especially those who can attract much younger men or their children's friends). Also *yummy mummy* and *Stacy's Mom.*

rejuvenile: Adult who enjoys activities normally associated with children.

Results for the Child of the Best Friend

If you manage to forge a best-friendship with your children, there's so much to look forward to in their adulthood. Created in your image, your best friends will be characterized by the following appealing traits:

- Either utterly without emotional boundaries, or with thick walls up to protect themselves from parental intrusions.

- Resentful that they had to grow up too quickly.

Parents Make the Party!

When you buy alcohol for your kids, you know they're getting it from a safe source *and* you get to join in on the fun! According to an American Medical Association study, almost 25 percent of teens have been supplied alcohol by their own parents and 40 percent by a friend's parent. Among the adults, 25 percent of parents feel teens should be able to drink at home with their parents present.

- Sexually promiscuous.

- Doubtful about the viability of marriage and close romantic relationships.

- Impaired work ethic, lack of discipline.

- Addicted to alcohol or drugs.

BFF!

"Best friends forever!" What could be better? Not only is this child flesh of your flesh, you'll never have to worry about social awkwardness again. The best-friend parenting type is one of the easiest to make up as you go along—just treat your child as you would an actual friend!

Next we turn to something completely different. In fact, you could even characterize it as "parent as enemy": the self-esteem killer. For those who have chosen the best-friend type, read on so you'll know what *not* to do. For others, however, this type will mesh perfectly with their unique parenting instincts!

VALIDATION IS FOR PARKING

8   PARENT AS SELF-ESTEEM KILLER

Life is tough, and the sooner your child figures out he's nothing special, the better. There's no free lunch, and you're not doing him any favors by falsely building up his touchy-feely self-esteem just so he can get it crushed in the real world. After all, you didn't get a leg up, so why should he? Better that he be prepared by having his family inform him he's worthless throughout his child-hood, so by the time it comes from a stranger, he'll have a thick skin. Once you commit to parenting via self-esteem homicide, you'll not only bestow a great gift on your offspring, you'll have a punching bag for the inevitable stresses of your own life.

Should You Be a Self-Esteem Killer?

As a self-esteem killer, you will have a special kinship with your children because you yourself have low self-esteem. Whether or not you're entirely aware of it, you loathe yourself deeply, a gift you plan to share with your child. Life has been a huge disappointment for you, and your child is no exception. Fortunately, she's young and can't defend herself, so she makes a perfect target for your pent-up feelings of failure. Unlike most of the people in your life, your child will believe you when you tell her how inadequate she is.

In general, parents' and children's self-esteem parallel one another, so the self-esteem killer is an ideal parenting choice for someone whose own parents killed their self-esteem. Self-esteem homicide tends to carry forward as a family legacy, so your own parents should be proud to see you carry on the family tradition!

Because the brief feelings of power that come with putting your children down don't last, this parenting type develops its own momentum. As with any deliberate parenting type, killing self-esteem takes work, but with a minimum of effort you'll find that it's easier and easier to spontaneously make your child feel terrible about herself.

Self-esteem homicide cross-pollinates beautifully with the controller, the pusher, the narcissist, and the neglector, so be sure to examine those sections for ways to deepen your ability to crush your child's spirit. You will gravitate toward self-esteem killing if you exhibit any of the following characteristics, behaviors, or beliefs, whether in parenting or in other aspects of your life, such as work or marriage:

- You have horrible luck. Others do nothing and get everything, while you have an inferior life that you didn't even choose.

- Everybody is out to get you.

- If only people acted right, you'd be able to relax.

- Your own parents didn't coddle you, that's for sure.

Don't Raise a Fatty

Who wants an overweight child? Fortunately, parents have a real partner in promoting the cult of thin—kids themselves. Almost half of girls in the first through third grades report wanting to be thinner. By their teens, half of girls and a quarter of boys have tried dieting. Of the girls, one in three don't even need to lose weight! Best of all, teens with low self-esteem are more likely to diet, so any preexisting self-esteem-killing parenting will only help further the cause. While children and teens who diet are far more likely to be overweight within five years as well as have disordered eating habits, at least by then they'll be out of the house and on their own.

Constantly Criticize, Never Praise

To toughen your child's skin and induce him to shape up, it's important to direct him with criticism. By all appearances, you've been cursed with a bumbling, stupid, ugly child. How dare he subject you to such inadequacy? The only way to get him back on track is to criticize him frequently and withhold praise. Criticism is best delivered in front of others, whether family, friends, or in public places, because humiliation will help your child learn.

Compare your child unfavorably to others, including siblings, friends, and people on television. Helpful words include "worthless," "good for nothing," and "idiot," especially when presented in a mocking tone. Never allow him to live down his mistakes, reminding him of them long after they've occurred. When in groups, regale others with stories of your child's idiocy; include a few such tales in your holiday family newsletter.

Don't Cut Your Child Any Slack

Just because your child is young doesn't mean she shouldn't be accountable for her ideas and actions. By knocking her down from the start, she will learn to question her own thoughts and understand that her opinions don't matter. If your child has an idea that's derivative or overly obvious, don't excuse it by saying it's smart "for a child." If it's dumb, it's dumb! When your child spills her orange juice, instead of chalking up her clumsiness to a lack of knowledge about gravity combined with undeveloped motor-muscle control, go ballistic and call her a clumsy oaf. If you begin making excuses for your child today, when will it stop? When she's a convicted felon?

Imagination Is an Unaffordable Luxury

When you're on the job, bringing home the bacon, do you have time or energy to exercise your imagination? Probably not. Life is hard and it demands pragmatic, realistic thinking, not tangerine trees and marmalade skies. You don't do your child any favors by encouraging sissy thinking. Besides, it's not like you can tell that drawing is of a horse, anyway.

Children have ridiculous senses of humor. They like knock-knock jokes and armpit-hand farting, and they can giggle about nothing for hours on end. Nip this in the bud by rolling your eyes or you'll find yourself with a kid who thinks he's better than everybody else. When your child comes to you requesting music or dance lessons, remind him that he can't carry a tune and there's no money for such frippery. Children are always developing interests that fade quickly, or worse, last a lifetime. Don't encourage him.

Promoting Sibling Rivalry

While parents play the key role in killing their children's self-esteem, siblings can also be enlisted in the effort. Here are some helpful guidelines for pitting siblings against one another:

1. Compare them to one another, especially unfavorably (e.g., "Why aren't you as smart as your brother?").

2. Pigeonhole them. One child could be "the pretty one," for example, while another is "the funny one."

3. Pick favorites. Every parent has one, so it's simply a matter of enacting the favoritism.

4. Avoid alone time with individual children, except when reinforcing favoritism.

5. Don't interfere in sibling fights, even if the older, larger sibling is physically attacking the younger, smaller sibling.

Curiously, the lower your child's self-esteem, the more likely it is he will become a writer.

You're Fat, You're Ugly

While physical attributes may not be the most important thing in the universe, we live in a looks-oriented world, and you never get a second chance to make a first impression. How badly it reflects on you to have a child who's less than perfect! In order to encourage her to keep up her looks, let her know what a disappointment she is to you. Whether it's acne, weight, bad hair, poor taste, facial features, or the ravages of puberty, impress upon your child how she fails to measure up in the looks department.

In this day and age, weight is the most important personal characteristic, more significant than character, morals, virtue, or intelligence. At the same time, childhood obesity is epidemic. Make sure your child knows that it is her number-one job to stay thin (whether or not you're able to accomplish this). You'd rather her grades suffer than her weight increase. Put her on a diet, restrict her favorite foods, and never pass up the opportunity to tell her she's a fat, unlovable slob.

Predict a Terrible Future

Happiness has been defined as the gap between expectation and reality. Your child will never amount to anything, so why set him up for disappointment? Whenever possible, remind your child that he has nothing to look forward to. Useful phrases include "You're worthless," "You'll never amount to anything," and "You're a complete disappointment to me." Someday your child will turn to you and say, "You were right all along." What a proud moment!

Stages of Self-Esteem Murder

1. **In utero:** Allow yourself to feel irritated at the inconveniences of pregnancy, reminding yourself that the baby is willfully causing indigestion, nausea, and sleeplessness (for mothers), not to mention inflicting a fat, whiny wife (for fathers). Wonder why the ultrasound depicts such an ugly fetus.

2. **Infant:** Tell your child to stop being such a cry-baby and wrinkle your nose in disgust when you must finally change a rancid diaper.

3. **Baby:** When your child spits up, yell at him for making a mess.

4. **Toddler:** With their clumsiness and tantrums, it's not hard to find plenty of opportunities to tell toddlers they're idiots.

5. **Child:** Once your child is in school, you can begin comparing him to others and gathering tangible proof of his stupidity.

6. **Adolescent:** Puberty brings physical changes that make any person look ugly—make sure these do not pass without comment.

7. **Teen:** In the teen years, referring to your child's bleak, useless future is especially effective.

8. **Young adult:** While watching your child flounder in the early stages of adulthood, say "I told you so" whenever possible.

9. **Adult:** Now that he's fully grown, let your child know there's no longer any doubt that he's a huge disappointment.

Tidings of Trauma

"Parents, you have caused my misfortune, and you have caused your own."

—**Arthur Rimbaud**

Results for the Child with No Self-Esteem

If you work hard to instill poor self-esteem in your children, there's so much to look forward to in their adulthood. Your self-hating offspring will be characterized by the following useful traits:

- Depressed, withdrawn, pessimistic.

- Fear of trying new things.

- Easily frustrated.

- Unable to find solutions for problems.

- Blame others for their problems.

- Exhibit "learned helplessness," passivity that results from repeated exposure to negative feedback and lack of belief in the possibility of making anything better.

- Quitters.

- Susceptible to peer pressure.

- Can become bullies in order to vent their negative feelings.

- Suicidal.

- Addicted to drugs and alcohol.

Self-Fulfilling Prophesies

The beauty of the self-esteem-killing approach is that it begets itself. While in your child's early years you will find yourself doing much of the work, soon enough she'll believe exactly what you tell her, and the burden of repeatedly telling her that she's worthless will dissipate.

In the next chapter, we will explore the seventh and final traumatic parenting type, the neglector. While the self-esteem killer actively instills negativity in children, the neglector can achieve similar results, as the effect of parental absence on children makes them feel unlovable.

DON'T
QUIT YOUR
DAY JOB

PARENT AS NEGLECTOR

Life is a complicated business. So many parents are busy working, socializing, or languishing under the bedcovers. Since it's likely that they themselves were neglected, these parents know that childhood neglect is no big deal. Even for those who weren't neglected, however, it's possible to learn and embrace these handy techniques, especially for fathers. When you neglect your children, you show them that they're not worthy of time or affection. Neglected children will learn to fend for themselves, sometimes reversing roles with their parents. For example, if you're a drinker, it's likely you can get your child to take care of *you*! There's no denying that neglect is the easiest parenting type there is, characterized not by the presence of behaviors you'll have to learn but instead by absence both physical and emotional.

Should You Be a Neglector?

So many individuals are well suited to be neglectful parents. Some neglectors choose addiction over their children. Others are depressed and emotionally unable to cope with the pressures of parenting. And many are so caught up in the rat race of career and social climbing that they don't feel they can take time to perform parenting functions themselves, deciding instead to outsource the work.

As with all the types, if you yourself were raised in the way you would like to parent (i.e., if you were neglected), you're going to have an easier time adopting the type's techniques. Neglectors tend to have difficulty with intimacy, and are uncomfortable revealing themselves to or

Dysfunctional Dictionary

cot potato: Baby or toddler who logs many hours in front of the television.

manny: Male nanny.

nanny envy: Parental jealousy over the amount of time the nanny gets to spend with the children.

screenager: Child who has grown up with screens, especially televisions and computers.

virtual visit: Child-parent interaction via webcams.

becoming dependent upon others. They can feel overwhelmed with the challenges of everyday life, feeling that the pressures of parenting bring yet another set of undesirable responsibilities. Sometimes they are enthusiasts who believe that every activity should be characterized by quality over quantity; after spreading themselves too thin, they convince themselves that parenting can take place in small, concentrated spurts. Overall, neglector parents tend to be self-absorbed and lack emotional maturity.

You will gravitate toward neglect if you exhibit any of the following characteristics, behaviors, or beliefs, whether in parenting or in other aspects of your life, such as work or marriage:

- It always seems like people want more from you than you're willing to give.

- You continually pledge to make significant changes after the next hurdle but never do so.

> **Tidings of Trauma**
>
> *"The place of the father in the modern suburban family is a very small one, particularly if he plays golf."*
>
> **—Bertrand Russell**

- You're already neglecting your spouse.

- You don't believe that children should affect your lifestyle.

Building Invisible Walls

Children are naturally affectionate, so in the early stages, it's important to communicate a "hands-off" message. Soon enough they'll absorb this ethos and keeping them away from you will be effortless. Hugging and kissing should always be kept to a minimum; not only is it uncomfortable for you, it breeds sissies and may cause taboo sexual tension.

The term "crybaby," of course, comes from children's tendency to cry easily over trivial injuries both real and perceived. If you give them attention for every little scratch, they won't develop the ability to soothe themselves. When you're busy, you're busy, and it's never too early for children to learn that they need to keep their problems to themselves if you're in the middle of something.

While at times it may feel difficult to deny your children affection, remind yourself that the walls you build today will turn into tomorrow's fortress around their hearts, so impenetrable that adult intimacy will prove all but impossible.

Emotional Disengagement

In addition to withholding affection from your children, it's vital to keep them feeling that they
don't know who you really are. Parents should
be mysteries to their children, inscrutable
and unpredictable ships passing in the night.
Whenever the opportunity arises to reveal
yourself to your child, squelch that urge. If your
child sees you as a human being, with feelings
and softness, not only will he take advantage
of you at every turn, you'll never have the chance
of seeming like a superhero in your child's eyes.
In a tough world, empathy is for chumps, and you
need to set the right hard-hearted example for
your offspring, giving them room to learn and
grow on their own.

Someone Has to Bring Home the Bacon

Children have no concept of the realities of life.
Where do they think food comes from? Who do
they think pays the rent? While they're whining
about their needs, do they ever acknowledge all

your efforts? Reconcile yourself to the fact that your children will never appreciate all that you do. When you stay late at work or your frequent business travel causes you to miss yet another school event, assuage your guilt by congratulating yourself for being a good provider. It's not like you left them with nothing to do: they've got the television, video games, and computers to keep them occupied. If they complain, tell them they're ungrateful brats.

Everybody Needs "Me" Time

Because your life is stressful, you must put your needs first. Whether it's frequent vacations, a frenetic social life, time spent cultivating high-level hygiene, or merely the servicing of an addiction, you need frequent breaks from your children to stay sane. Someday, when they're parents themselves, they'll understand what it's like. In the meantime, don't reject any opportunities or change your lifestyle in order to be a parent. Because children lack perspective, they will never understand your needs, so it's up to you to honor them.

Outsourced Parenting

Fortunately for the neglector, there are many resources to make sure that children don't physically harm themselves in your absence. With a wide range of options as well as costs, you're certain to find the solution that's right for you.

School Away from Home

For the busy parent, boarding school is an excellent way to balance lifestyle with the demands of a child. When children go away to school, they are only underfoot during holidays and occasional weekends, when it's possible to find babysitters for much of the time.

Most people think of boarding school as an alternative only for teens, but in the United States, boarding schools start at the third-grade level. This is more in keeping with the British tradition, which has always started early; nowadays, many British institutions accept seven-year-olds.

Why wait until a child is a discipline problem requiring military or wilderness school? Tuition and board may average almost $60,000 per year, but the freedom parents gain is priceless.

For the affluent, nannies and boarding school are excellent options. Live-in nannies provide far more child care for the investment and save you from having to schedule different babysitters for evening outings. In many cases, children end up preferring their nannies, which takes pressure off parents.

Those who can't afford full-time help or boarding schools often use day care. Most preschools and child care facilities offer extra services to extend your child's stay, so you can cobble together as many as twelve daily hours to have the kids off your hands. You can also try leaving your children with friends, neighbors, or relatives, whether regularly or on an ad hoc basis. Even if you don't return when you say you will, these caregivers will rarely turn your child out onto the streets.

Finally, television makes an excellent babysitter. Most children are happy to spend hours in front of the television, so if you want to go out for a while, just put the remote in their hands and show them how to help themselves to soda from the fridge.

Better Living Through Chemistry

Does your child run wild around the house? Do you have trouble keeping up with his antics? Is he sad, moody, or "creative"? Rather than spending unnecessary time with your child, give yourself a break and let modern medication step in. The perks are quite compelling!

Your child will fit in with his peers. In the United States alone, over five million children have been diagnosed with ADHD (Attention-Deficit/Hyperactivity Disorder). Of those children with a current diagnosis, over two-thirds are taking medication for the disorder. And as of 2010, up to eight million children take one— or more!—psychotropic drugs.

Your child will be on trend. A recent study asserts that five times as many high school and college students in the United States are dealing with anxiety and other mental health issues compared to young people who were studied in the 1930s—ironically, the era of the Great Depression.

Your child will hone his acting skills. A 2010 study in the scientific journal *Psychological Assessment* indicated that ADHD symptoms (and test results!) can be quite easily feigned with a cursory knowledge of the disorder. Practice makes perfect!

Stages of Neglect

1. **In utero:** Don't bother changing your diet or smoking, drinking, and drug habits just because you're pregnant. For fathers, pregnancy is an ideal time to leave without a forwarding address.

2. **Infant:** Because your child can't yet get herself out of the crib, go out and run some errands when you've put her down for a nap. If you run into a friend, find a café or bar and settle in for a long chat!

3. **Baby:** Babies can be very demanding. Use this opportunity to set your child straight by letting her know that crying will get her nowhere.

4. **Toddler:** Toddlerhood marks the beginning of a lifelong love affair with the television. Because there aren't enough hours of children's programming, get your toddler started on adult shows as early as possible.

5. **Child:** Finally—your child can feed herself and move around the neighborhood on her own two feet. Let her.

6. **Adolescent:** Only discipline your adolescent if she annoys you; otherwise, let her explore the world on her own. Chances are she'll be out of the house more often than she's at home, making adolescence a very freeing time for the parent.

7. **Teen:** For the wealthy, boarding school is now an option. Or you can try juvenile detention facilities, which are free.

8. **Young adult:** Now that your child is on her own, make some demands on her, whether for money or respect.

9. **Adult:** Watch with pride as your child neglects her own children!

Results for the Neglected Child

If you do very little to raise your children, there's so much to look forward to in their adulthood. Your laissez-faire offspring will be characterized by the following inimitable traits:

- Needy and dependent, or problems with intimacy and emotional attachments.

- Grow up too fast, experiment with sex and drugs.

- Low self-esteem, feeling unworthy of love or happiness.

- Attention-seeking troublemakers.

- Seek out withholding, emotionally absent relationships.

- Anger issues, frequent fighting, aggressive.

- Depressed.

- Caretaking at the expense of self-care.

- Problems with discipline and work ethic.

- Pessimistic.

- Drug and alcohol addiction, eating disorders.

> ### 💬 Tidings of Trauma
>
> *"Kids are the best . . . You can teach them to hate the things you hate. And they practically raise themselves, what with the Internet and all."*
> **—Homer Simpson**

After Childbirth, Your Job Is Done!

You gave them life—what more do they want? You have your own life to enjoy. Fortunately, when you neglect your children, they learn compensatory techniques for self-sufficiency, and in the meantime, you get to accomplish everything you set out to do. Restraint is the name of this game, and after some practice, you'll be withholding with the best of them.

Congratulations on taking this journey through the seven traumatic parenting types. Parenting has its ups and downs, and now that you're armed with the knowledge to traumatize your children deliberately, there's no end to the possibilities!

ENJOYING YOUR LEGACY OF TRAUMA

10

CONCLUSION

You thought this day would never come: your children are grown and out of the house (or, in some cases, still living with you into their thirties and forties). While parenting is truly a lifelong endeavor, the critical period of responsibility is behind you. No longer do you need to focus on inflicting trauma—instead, you can sit back and watch the results unfold. Raising children is like growing a garden: you have no idea what the oak tree is going to look like when you plant the acorn in the soil. In your old age, however, you've earned the privilege of sitting in the leafy shade, and, if you've done the job correctly, you can hammer nails in the tree and build the treehouse of your retirement.

Never Explain, Never Justify

All children look back on their childhood and wish their parents had done something differently. No matter the traumatizing approach you chose, your children will wish you'd gone another way, especially when they enter therapy. Don't give in to this kind of Monday-morning quarterbacking. Hindsight is 20-20, and it's all too easy to close the barn door after the horse has left the stable.

Deflect Blame

When your children complain about something you did years ago, *never* take responsibility for it. If you want to seem insightful, take the blame for something irrelevant that never actually affected them, but tell them you have no idea why they're whining about whatever it is that seems to matter to them. Finally, try

Tidings of Trauma

"Like all parents, my husband and I just do the best we can, and hold our breath, and hope we've set aside enough money to pay for our kids' therapy."

—**Michelle Pfeiffer**

returning the blame to them—if they hadn't been so stupid, shallow, or disobedient, you wouldn't have had to do what you did.

Remind Them of Their Responsibilities to You

Now that they're adults, it's time for your children to cut you some slack and start supporting you. This is the cycle of life—just as you (or the nanny) changed their diapers, so one day will they change yours. Guilt is an excellent tool for instilling this type of responsibility—inflict it as heavily as possible, reminding them repeatedly of how much you sacrificed for them.

Tidings of Trauma

"Parents wonder why the streams are bitter, when they themselves have poisoned the fountain."
—**John Locke**

Don't Be Offended If They Choose a Different Approach

It's the nature of parenting that your children are likely to choose a different approach to traumatizing when they themselves have families. While at first blush it's easy to be offended that they didn't think highly enough of your choices to repeat them, remember that once upon a time you read this book and carefully selected a traumatizing style for yourself. Rather than lambasting their unique choice, revel in parental pride for instilling in your children the traumatizing instinct. Your grandchildren will thank you one day!